Selections from

"A Star is Born"

MUSIC BY HAROLD ARLEN   LYRICS BY IRA GERSHWIN

SONGS

Illustrated with pictures from the
Warner Bros. Cinemascope and Technicolor production

As sung by Judy Garland in her new starring picture "A STAR IS BORN"

The Man That Got Away

Tune Ukulele A D F♯ B

Lyric by
IRA GERSHWIN

Music by
HAROLD ARLEN

As sung by Judy Garland in her new starring picture "A STAR IS BORN"

It's A New World

Lyric by
IRA GERSHWIN

Tune Ukulele A D F#B

Music by
HAROLD ARLEN

Refrain *with warmth and grandeur*

It's a new world I see ____

A new world for me! ____

The tears ____ have rolled off my cheek ____

And fears ____ fade a - way ev - 'ry time you speak. ____

As sung by Judy Garland in her new starring picture A STAR IS BORN

Someone At Last

Lyric by
IRA GERSHWIN

Tune Ukulele F B♭ D G

Music by
HAROLD ARLEN

As sung by Judy Garland in her new starring picture "A STAR IS BORN"

Gotta Have Me Go With You

Lyric by
IRA GERSHWIN

Tune Ukulele A D F#B

Music by
HAROLD ARLEN

Moderato

Verse

What_ a spot, this_ Not_ so hot, this!_ Hey_ there

shy one_ Come_ be my one!_ Please_ don't rush off_

Want_ no brush off_ I can't com - pel you to buy what I'd sell you But

I've got to tell you like so:

Chorus *(Steadily - with much excitement)*

You wan-na have bells that -'ll ring, You wan-na have songs that -'ll sing? You want your sky a ba - by blue? You got-ta have me go with you. Hey,___ you fool you___ Why___ so cool you___ When___ I'm rea - dy___ To___ go

As sung by Judy Garland in her new starring picture "A STAR IS BORN"

Lose That Long Face

Tune Ukulele A D F♯ B

Lyric by
IRA GERSHWIN

Music by
HAROLD ARLEN

Moderato

Verse *(Lightly)*

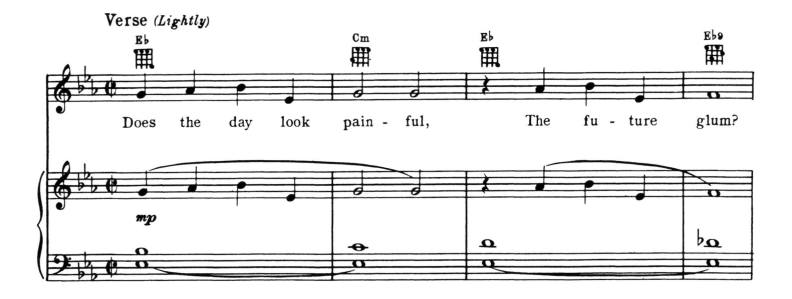

Does the day look pain - ful, The fu - ture glum?

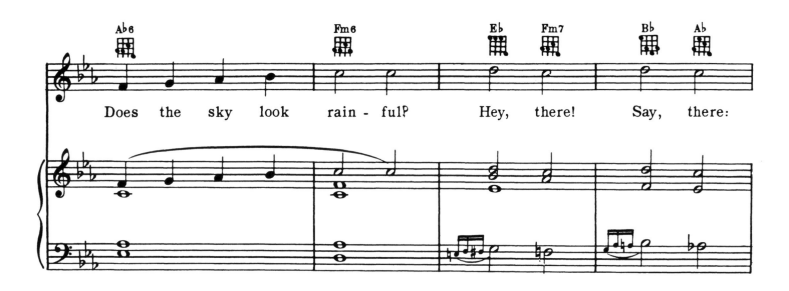

Does the sky look rain - ful? Hey, there! Say, there:

Are you in a va-cu-um? All this stuff and non-sense You can o-ver-come. A long face gets you no-where; You lose That Month of May. Like Pe-ter Pan, the sweet-er pan Wins the day.

As sung by Judy Garland in her new starring picture "A STAR IS BORN"

Here's What I'm Here For

Lyric by
IRA GERSHWIN

Tune Ukulele A D F#B

Music by
HAROLD ARLEN

Slowly *(with expression)*

What am I here for? It's time you knew.

Here's what I'm here for: I'm here for you.

Can you for - give me? Am I too late?